THE
PENDULUM
BOOK

by

Hanna Kroeger

Table of Contents

FOREWORD

Knowingly or unknowingly, everyone has a sixth sense. It is more developed in some than in others. Children have it more than adults and old folks often regain the ability of their childhood knowledge pertaining to the sixth sense.

Every one of our five senses can be used constructively or destructively. There are people who only see and hear evil and others who never see the snakes and beetles. They are absorbed in the beauty of a rose and do not feel the sting of the thorns.

There are people who feel gloomy all day long and others feel the sunshine on their skin and absorb it.

So it is with the sixth sense. Just invite the cleanest consciousness with the sixth sense. Christ said "I stand at the door and knock." Please use your sixth sense to open the door for Him!

The great University of Occult Knowledge is open now and Christ is our President.

We are coming from many walks of life; we are drawn together under the banner of the Light Bearers of the Aquarian Age.

Like every student in a university, we have to work hard and diligently to learn the lessons given to us.

So learn to use them in the spirit of this university and in the spirit of its President.

CHAPTER ONE

The first time I learned about the pendulum was through Linda Clark, famous author on nutrition. In her book, *Get Well Naturally,* she describes how her friends used the pendulum, and there is where it all started for me. I took my wedding ring and hung it on a thread, dangling it over my hands, my knees and my food and, sure enough, slowly, slowly the ring started gyrating. I steadied myself in every way possible but the ring was moving.

For one year I worked on this phenomenon, not showing it to anyone but my closest friends. I ordered books printed in England, France and America. I found writings in the Bible about it. I talked to prominent women, to doctors, to psychologists, but no one could give me the answers I was searching for. Why does a pendulum work? Which energies are there involved? And many more questions.

By using the pendulum I found out that I could live a healthier life by picking out my food with it. One day I found that my mind could control the swing of the pendulum. That was the day when I almost gave up this art. What use did a phenomenon have when I could control it with my mind?

That one day—it was a marvelous spring day—I was going over some flowers, just budding close to the ground. I checked them with the pendulum to find out what rate of vibration the petals, the leaves and the roots had, when suddenly in all the peace and sunshine I felt as if a hand lay on mine and the words came to my mind. "Let go and let God." I relaxed, I went into my innermost and at once the pendulum gyrated differently, accurately, exactly. I found the key: "Let go and let God," and I have followed this advice since. Some people do not use the pendulum. Many are using a rod, a reed or a stick as it is advised in the Bible. Others sit in front of a candle and, surprisingly enough, the flame answers their questions by bending forward, sideward, backward and by twisting or shaking one way or another. The American Indians find their herbal remedies with their sacred stick. We visited the Sioux Indians and graciously they invited us to take part in their herb hunting. The chief, who is also the spiritual leader, walked with the sacred stick which is a painted and decorated rod with one delicate feather tied on each end of the stick. We slowly walked over the hills when the lower feather, the one close to the ground, started to straighten out while the other one was limply hanging. The chief changed his steps to the way the feather was pointing. When the other feather started to straighten out, he halted. The upper feather, now pointing the same direction as the lower one, whipped five times. The chief took five steps and stood in front of a measly looking dried up plant. "Great medicine," he said.

His helpers came with a shovel and spade and worked for over one hour to dig out the largest root I'd ever seen. It looked like a bottle. "Great medicine," the chief said, after he had sprinkled some tobacco in the hole, blessing the place where the root was dug out.

What had moved the feathers? There was no wind. Why did one feather straighten out and not the other? The chief, with a convincing smile, said "It is the Great Spirit."

CHAPTER TWO

The rod, the reed and the staff are mentioned many times in the Bible. It was used extensively in those days to guide and measure, to bring water (Moses) and to lead the nations. The Pharaohs used it (Exodus 7:8-25). Maybe Moses learned the use of the rod from them. Among the Pharaohs this secret was very much guarded. The oldest known picture of dowsing was found in the ruins of Mesopotamia (1300 B.C.) where a priest is pictured using a forked divining rod. During the Dark Ages the use of the rod or pendulum fell in disrespect because the churches and their leaders had the funny idea to suppress their subjects and members rather than to help them. The use of the pendulum and the rod has its resurrection now. We have to turn back to the days of old to survive.

We cannot send every apple into the laboratories to find out if it is DDT drenched or arsenic sprayed or both but we can apply the art of using the pendulum the right way to find out if the apple is poisoned or fit to eat. We cannot send every piece of meat to an inspector to find out whether or not it has trichinae or hormone residue. But we can use our pendulum to find out if the meat is good for us or not. By the way, for years Cal-Tech was teaching the use of the pendulum to especially bright and interested graduate students. So let's join the smart and intelligent crowd and use the pendulum.

First of all, while learning the use of the pendulum or the use of the rod, you must establish your own personal pattern. Hold your pendulum between your palms in order to warm it up with your vibrations. When borrowing a pendulum from someone else this is very important. You have to make the stone or rod neutral from vibrations and warm it up, so to speak, with your own personality.

Remember how in school we were taught that we are running on a low, subdued electrical charge; that we are a battery running on acids and alkaline juices clear down to the very dynamo of our smallest cell unit?

The middle finger is of a positive charge, the forefinger is negative and the thumb checks neutral. As we go on you must keep these facts in your mind.

Here is the method I teach:

Hold the chain or string of the pendulum about 2 to 3 inches above the stone or ring or dangling object. You hold it in your right hand between thumb, forefinger and middle finger (Trinity). Bring it over your middle finger of the left hand and ask "Which is my positive pattern?" Slowly, the pendulum will start moving back and forth, sideways or gyrating one way or another. Keep your question in your mind about the positive pattern and this day practice only this one aspect of movement many times until you establish firmly in your subconscious mind the pattern of your positive pendulum swing. Do not be influenced by others saying the pendulum has to swing clockwise or so. You are you, and you have your personal lifestyle and your individual pendulum swing.

The next day try your negative pattern. Hold the pendulum over your left forefinger and ask "Which is my negative pattern?" Again it will start to move, this time in a different direction, indicating your negative vibrational pattern. This is your "no" pattern. When food is poisonous to you or you are allergic to some parts of it, it will swing the no pattern and it is up to you to eat it or leave it alone. Please do not be in such a rush. Again take your time. You have to establish in your makeup your negative indicator. Work on it one full day, asking, working and praying, and don't forget the thanking. Do it until you are ready for your last swing.

Hold the pendulum over your thumb and wait for your neutral pattern to come. The pendulum may stand still or swing back and forth. At any rate it is your neutral pattern. Food which checks neutral does not hurt you nor adds energies to your system. Truly you are of spiritual nature.

4

Please do not be unhappy when your pendulum does not swing the very first time you try it. Good things often have to be acquired. Notice that the more effort it will take a student to learn the art, the more appreciative they become after they find out they can do it. Many of my friends who did not have much luck the first 50 times they tried it became my best and most reliable pendulum users.

Notice: When you try to use the pendulum the very first time and it stands dead still, lay it aside and stand with feet apart. Stretch your left arm to the north and your right arm to the south and stand this way a minute or two. You do this in order to increase the magnetic forces flowing through you from north to south.

Now, with your hands stroke down your body briskly several strokes at a time. Start at the right side of the head, brush with the left hand the right arm from shoulders down, then with both hands from the right hip to the right toe. Then over the face, the chest, the front of both legs. Then with the right hand brush the left side of face, left arm, with both hands from the left hip down to the left foot. This is a method with which you make yourself ready for more flow of magnetic energy. You become an instrument of the paranormal, which are energies beyond the measurable.

Now try your pendulum again. If this will not help, hold the pendulum over your right knee. The knees emit more electromagnetic power than the fingers do and you may get some movement of your pendulum by doing this. If not, hold it over your left knee and try that. Often times the mistake is made to hold the pendulum on too long a string or chain. Place your fingers about 2 inches above the stone, then try again.

Now if it still does not move, set it aside and before you go to bed, meditate about it. Feel the forces going through your body. Feel them going to your fingertips. Feel the movements. Feel your body filling up with vibrations. Then go to sleep. The next day, try again and the next day again. It will come. The more effort you put into it the more exciting will be the results.

Many people using the pendulum with ease put it far too soon aside saying I can do it when I want to. Others who had a hard time to begin with stuck with it and soon surpassed everyone else in accuracy and performance.

Now after you find that the pendulum will and can swing, you will make the remarkable discovery that your mind can move it. You can move it at will and the swing will obey your command. Your thoughts can influence the swing of the pendulum in any direction you wish—positive, negative or neutral.

Pause and admire the grandeur and largesse of your mind. You are capable of influencing a dead object to move with your mind. You can oscillate and gyrate it, you can make it halt so it stands still, just to start it up with your thoughts again. Thoughts are things created in the astral dimensions, taking form and making appearances in the third dimension, the visible realm. Think how powerful thoughts are. When you lose the train of thought, trace back your steps to the place you lost it and sure enough it is sitting on your workbench, the table or the shelf waiting to be picked up like a forgotten puppy.

You lost your car keys. In your mind trace back where you used them last and they are right next to the cookie jar. (You had been disappointed and needed a sweet uplift.) Always stay in full control of your mental capacity, and of your thoughts. Never have destructive thoughts—no hate, no fear—so "it will not come upon you," as the Bible said in Isaiah 47:10–12. This is the first lesson the pendulum work teaches you—the power of thought. It would be a good idea for you to sign up in a mind control course to learn more about the subject. Also read the book *Your Mind Can Heal You* and similar publications. However, we are not interested in showing what the mind can do. We want to learn to use the pendulum and here is your third lesson.

The first lesson was moving the pendulum.

The second lesson was mind control.

The third lesson is contacting the super conscious in order to conduct our lives according to the orders and the laws of God. Therefore, before you go any further with the plays and the powers of the mind, remember "The Lord is my Shepherd, I shall not want." I shall keep my little ego out of the way. I shall keep my ever creative thoughts under control until I have asked my inner guidance – until I have asked Jesus the Christ for his opinion – "the Great Spirit Guidance," as Indians told me, "the innermost," "the Holy of the Holiest." When you use the art of the pendulum you "Let go and let God." This alone is the secret of success. Let go and let your deepest subconscious, the super conscious, solve the problem. The subconscious is connected with the higher planes, the higher powers, the "knowers," the sublime. And your most honest prayers, your true meditations, bring you in contact with these heavenly forces which help you and guide you. They teach you over and over again. They forgive your shortcomings if you honestly try to overcome. They surround you by day and by night. "Without Him we cannot do anything."

I can understand that the art of dowsing or divining was anxiously guarded by the priesthood because of the fact that it takes more than the movement of the pendulum to do this art right. But the New Age, the Aquarian Age, is coming. People are ready for this work. Once I tell my students about the sacredness of the art of divining, they understand and never use it incorrectly.

It is a long way from the first movement of the pendulum to the place where you are ready to "Let go and let God." It took me one year. If it takes you just as long, which I doubt very much, work, be patient and trust. Every time I sit down to take vibrational counts of one object or another I ask first for permission, second for guidance and third for advice. And believe me, God knows it all. Of course, I make mistakes when emotions overrun me. It is very difficult to help beloved ones when my ego goes on show instead of minding its own affairs, when I am physically tired or not in harmony with the universe. But it is me who makes costly, tiresome and stupid mistakes and not the Lord, believe me. I learned to get up at 3 or 4 A.M. for meditation and pendulum work. Then, in the peace of the dawning day, I feel closest to God and the correct interpretation of the divine.

CHAPTER THREE

PENDULUM AND SCIENCE

I.

We live in 3 worlds of vibrations.

The first manifestation of vibration is physical and is expressed in:

- feeling
- subsonic sound
- audible sound
- supersonic sound

The media through which these manifestations are transmitted are:

- gas
- liquids
- solids

The speed of transmission through this media is:

- 1100 feet per second (fps) in air
- The speed in liquid or solid media varies based on density, temperature, chemical composition and other factors.

Physicists and scientists have instruments to measure the physical existence of above vibrations.

II.

The second manifestation of vibration is electromagnetic in nature and expresses in:

- low frequency electrical
- radio broadcast
- high frequency radar
- infrared
- ultraviolet rays
- cosmic rays

The medium through which these vibrations are transmitted is:

- ether

The speed of transmission through this medium is:
- approximately 185,000 miles per second (the speed of light)

It was in 1975 that scientists declared that the human body has an electromagnetic system with circuits and outlets. The above mentioned vibrations used this electromagnetic system. Even though it is possible for the scientists to measure these vibrations outside the body, it is not possible as yet to measure these frequencies in the human body with the conventional methods and conventional instruments.

The human body has organs which transform the electromagnetic waves so that the impact is buffered. These organs are the holy chakras. There are 9 chakras in a Western man and 7 in an Eastern man.

III.

The third manifestation of vibration is astral-etheric in nature. It is called *Higher Dimensional Energies*, in short HD, and expresses in:
- aura emanation
- eloptic emanation
- meditation
- prayer
- ESP
- emotion
- thought

The medium through which these vibrations are transmitted is:
- *Akasha* or *Nieonic*

The speed of transmission through this medium is:
- instantaneous

To measure astral-etheric vibrations, physicists and chemists, including biochemists, are not equipped to do so. They do not have the proper instruments to measure etheric vibrations. Even the De La Warr's Radionic Instruments need an operator with well developed ESP.

9

Intuition comes from a higher realm. Intuition is the language of the soul. If you could find an instrument with which you could ask your soul directly, would that not be a fantastic invention? Such an instrument exists. It is the pendulum with which you can converse with your all knowing soul. (Your soul is always in connection with higher intelligence—with God.) You ask your soul with your pendulum and you will receive the answer through your pendulum.

Some scientists will admit that there are aura emanations. Some will admit that there is power in mantras and power in prayers. However, scientists do not have an instrument which will measure the output of an earnest prayer. There is no gadget that can measure a prayer in numbers or weight or angstroms. Therefore, scientists may deny the existence of these powers. They may deny the reading of an aurameter, a psychometric reading, and will ridicule the use of a dowsing rod.

Many people say that what scientists cannot measure does not exist. That is not so. The foundation on which science stands is the rational materialistic realm. The prayer of a soul and the purity of a heart is a field beyond rational, materialistic view. They are realms of higher nature.

IV.

In many states of the US radiesthesia is still a public no-no. This is hard to believe since radiesthesia is widely and publicly used in France, England, Germany and Russia. Particularly France, with her great son and pioneer Abbe Mermet, is way ahead in psychometric knowledge. And yet, it is in America where the greatest breakthrough into the realization of these astral-etheric vibrations was made. Scientists found that the nerves are the transmitters of vibrations mentioned in Section I above. In 1975 the electromagnetic web below the skin was recognized to be able to transmit energies mentioned in Section II above.

In 1908 researchers at Harvard University came up with astounding news. They found that certain energies enter our bodies through the pores of the skin, go through endless nadis or

10

channels and gather in 33 centers. I want to make sure that we understand that these higher energies are not electromagnetic in nature, they are not using the chakras as transformers. They are finer in nature. These energies are the true healers.

Through these nadis and centers the intuition flows. As I stated, the intuition is the language of the soul and the pendulum, the rod and radiesthesia are the instruments with which you can measure and verify and interpret the language of your soul and come in contact with the all knower.

At Harvard the research was dropped since they had no practical use for it.

CHAPTER FOUR

By experience I know that many, many people do not go along with me when I teach the use of the pendulum. They say it is the devil's work. I wonder what our forefathers would have said 150 years ago when they saw a television set flashing pictures into the peace of their family life? Wouldn't they have said "this is the devil at work?" (Sometimes I say this when the pictures are too bad.) It is all misunderstanding of forces surrounding us. First, I will tell you what the Bible has to say about this subject of the rod because the priesthood has been using the divining rod all along.

In Exodus 4:17 we read "And thou shalt take this rod in thine hand, wherewith thou shalt do signs." To my surprise I found that the scepter of the king is a replica of the rod which was to be used in leading the people. Numbers 17:2 tells us about it. And Jehovah spoke unto Moses saying, "Speak unto the children of Israel and take rods, one for each father's house. To all the princes according to their father's house." In Exodus 4:20 "And Moses took his wife and his sons, and set them upon an ass, and he returned to the land of Egypt: and Moses took the rod of God in his hand." This is a sign that the rod was used quite openly. The Bible also tells us what kind of rod was used. In Jeremiah 1:11 "Moreover the word of the Lord came unto me, saying, Jeremiah, what seest thou? And I said, I see a rod of an almond tree." Then said the Lord "Thou hast well seen: for I will hasten my word to perform it." In Micah 7:14 we hear about the command "Feed thy people with the rod ... ." This order is good enough for all housewives to get busy and pick out the unsprayed, wholesome and healthy food from the preserved and adulterated food. The same seer Micah said "Thou wilt perform the truth to Jacob, and the mercy to Abraham, which thou hast sworn unto our fathers from the days of old." It means we shall be using the pendulum or rod as in the days of old. Revelation 11:1 cautions us that even our church associations should be measured, "And there was given me a reed like unto a rod: and the angel stood, saying, Rise, and measure the temples of God, and the altar, and them that worship therein." The rod was considered so important and holy that it had its place in the Holy of Holiest. Hebrews 9:3-4 "And after the second veil, the tabernacle which is called the Holiest of all; Which had the golden censer, and the ark of the covenant overlaid round about with gold, wherein was the golden pot that had manna, and Aaron's rod that budded, and the tables of the covenant."

Only the high priests were allowed to enter this sanctuary to use the rod and speak to God. Manna, by the way, are wheat sprouts presenting the life force and power in each grain used physically as well as spiritually.

In Isaiah 10:5 it is shown that the rod will not work when one is in anger, "O, Assyrian, the rod of mine anger, and the staff in their hand is mine indignation."

I want to impress upon you the word of Ezekiel 20:37. "And I will cause you to pass under the rod, and I will bring you into the bond of the covenant." That means you are bound to God in a sacred promise to do His work.

We are heavily warned not to misuse the rod and the pendulum in Deuteronomy 18:10–12. It says whosoever doeth these things going through fire, which means using the dark forces. Enchanting a sorcerer, consulting of Nec, using divination, is an abomination unto Jehova.

Never use the pendulum for speculation, to gain power over others, for prediction and what not. It is a device of measurement and one that uses it correctly is under the covenant of the Most High, as the Bible said.

CHAPTER FIVE

WHICH ENERGIES MOVE THE PENDULUM?

I have been asked many, many times what is it that moves the pendulum? Which are the powers that gyrate, swing or stop a pendulum? Which are the energies involved in dowsing, in radiesthesia, in dermo-optical perception and other paranormal experiences?

In my opinion, all these phenomena show that the unseen is stronger than the seen. The powers which create are more powerful than the creation. The Master is wiser than the students.

Before going into details, we have to make some groundwork so we understand the meaning of some words better.

Psychometry comes from the Greek word *psukhe* or *psyche* which means soul and *metron* which means measure. In other words, psychometry is measuring the expressions of the psyche of an object of any kind. You can measure the psyche of the flowers, the stones, the herbs, the animal kingdom, parts of the animal kingdom, the human body and also parts of it. Everything is vibration. Every star, every root, every flower, every seed has its own electromagnetic charge and gives it off, spends it freely. Every creation of the Lord has its own harmonious singing.

There is another word you have to know about—*psychoscopy*. Psychoscopy is a modern version of the word psychometry. So when you read the word, psychoscopist, you know that this is a man or woman who has the gift to tell a great deal about a subject by touching or by using the pendulum.

You have to know about another word. It is *radiesthesia*. Again, this word is derived from the Greek and it means "rod" or "divining." The modern man does not carry a mystic wand or rod or reed around but you never know in whose pocket is hidden a pendulum.

14

I gave a talk at a congregation of a Lutheran Church. By mistake I had left my pendulum at home and when I needed it for demonstration, many of the congregation assembled had one handy.

Why don't we call our pendulum a psychometer? This is the correct word for it. It is an instrument to measure vibrations emanating from an object or being.

The psychometer is not an instrument to make predictions. Predictions come through seeing and knowing which is the highest of all psychic phenomena, the prophetic one.

It is the seer in the Old Testament who predicted and saw future events. The coming of Christ was predicted and seen long before He was born. So were our current events seen and recorded.

The basis of radiesthesia is the basis of all paranormal phenomena with the exception of prophesy. The famous scientist Michael Faraday said "All matter is composed of atoms vibrating at different rates of speed to form different densities."

Whatever power the matter possesses, it owes it to the type of electrical charge or vibration given off by the substance.

That means every object radiates energies—the table, the chair, the flower on the window sill, the dog lying on the carpet. Actually, we live in a sea of energies like a fish lives in an ocean and is carried by the water. So we live in an ocean of energy and forces and without them we could not exist.

A psychoscopist is capable of tuning in to some of these energies which are emanated from the material world around him and, through training, he will be able to translate these vibrations into something we need to know.

For example, in water dowsing the psychoscopist with his forked rod (or straight one) tunes in to the vibration of water beneath the surface of the earth. He picks up the psyche of the water, the fork bends down and the dowser is able to tell by experience and his inner awareness how deep the underground stream is located, how much water is present and many more particulars about the water beneath the earth.

15

The same is true when hunting for minerals, herbs, lost objects or lost people. The psychoscopist tunes in to the subject or object and its emanation and can tell about this subject all he has to know because he is contacting the psyche of the object, the aura, the blueprint, and not the materialization of the third dimension of the given thing or person.

Everything material also has an unseen blueprint in another dimension and it is this blueprint which is contacted by a psychoscopist or clairvoyant.

We would be in a terrible mass of stagnant vibrations, good, bad or indifferent, if The Creator would not have taken care of this in advance. He put a powerful force over the earth, the magnetic stream, which goes from north to south. This force stirs up the stagnant vibrations of the huge cities and nullifies or cleans them without our doings.

The magnetic forces orbiting the earth from north to south are also penetrating us. We truly are a "child of the universe." We take part of this force, a force that is helping, harmonizing, invigorating and sustaining us.

This stream enters our bodies predominantly through the left hand, left ear, left hip and left foot. It takes its path through the nervous system to reenter the earth flow through the right hand, right hip and right foot.

You ask me why? God made it this way so that we may become a part of His tremendously powerful creation.

The magnetic force field is the carrier of two vital forces: the life force and the odic force.

Every creation on this earth takes part in the life force. It is given to the unborn. It is in the sprouting grain. It holds the stone together so that it will not fall to dust. You and I dine daily and every minute on this field of life force which is carried to us by the magnetic power field encircling the earth from north to south continually.

When someone is a dynamic person, he has opened himself to lots of life force energy and is able to dine more freely and copiously on this manna. Lots of magnetic energies flow

16

through these people. When he or she is founded in God, it is a joy to be around them.

As I mentioned, the magnetic force field is also the carrier of another mighty important force field, the odic force.

The odic force enters the body the same way as the magnetic one does, mainly through the left side of the body.

Behind the breastbone we have a small gland, the thymus gland. It has many functions. One of them is to transform the odic force to a power which your individual body can handle. The odic power is your brain sensitizer. It has its main concentration between the frontal lobes on the forehead where the Indian women and men wear the red, white or turquoise spot or a jewel.

Some people have a greater receptive capacity in the forehead for the odic force field than others. It was found that in gifted healers the frontal lobes were further apart than in others. These people naturally have more healing powers. This does not mean that you could not train yourself for the same performance!

It is this odic force which carries your personal impressions—your thoughts, your worries, your physical and other ailments, your joy and your prayers are carried back into the magnetic field of your surroundings. And this odic force is the vibration which the pendulum picks up.

I have seen highly sensitive people who, by holding your pencil in their hands, could tell all about you, your happiness, your physical troubles and your personality because the pencil still had your odic impressions on it.

Now you understand why the pendulum works. There is no magic to it, no black force.

We and we alone were so limited that we did not recognize the unseen forces surrounding us.

Jesus said "You do not live from bread alone." Finally we catch on. Jesus forgive us that it took us so long to understand Your words. It took us 2,000 years to realize how these divine force fields carry us, nourish us and keep us going.

Einstein said "Energy and matter are interchangeable." The unseen energies move the rod, the reed, the pendulum.

Now it is up to us to read and translate these energies correctly and only you who are founded in God's faith will do a good job.

CHAPTER SIX

After you have learned the use of the pendulum you will never be without one. Some people will prefer a willow rod or an iron or a hazelnut rod over this pendulum but a pendulum is so handy.

Some people have it attached to their favorite pin. It hides in a spectacle case, it has a secure place in a pocketbook. It may be attached to your car key. I carry mine in my apron pocket.

The practical uses of the pendulum are as manifold as your imagination will allow you to expand.

Here are some practical uses:

Go shopping with it. I do and I have great results.

Place you left hand over the packages and dangle your pendulum over it or inconspicuously on your side and ask silently:

Is this free from preservatives?

It this cottage cheese fresh?

Is this milk drenched with formaldehyde?

Is this a fair buy?

You go to the meat counter. There are 20 chickens on display. All seem alike but your sixth sense will soon find out. Ask which chicken is fit to eat. Usually there will be one or two over which the pendulum will gyrate with a positive swing. Just to convince yourself, take a positive chicken and a negative chicken and cook them at the same meal in separate dishes and let your family decide!

Ask for the best buy on meats. "Is this piece of meat from an animal treated with hormones?"

At the fruit counter ask:

"Are these apples sprayed with pesticides?"

"Is this lettuce good for us?"

"Are the tomatoes fit to eat?"

You will be surprised that some cans of fruit are excellent while with others the pendulum says no. I found that the cheaper asparagus are better than the high priced ones. In eggs it makes a huge difference in taste alone. Definitely ask your wand when you come to the cheese display.

For the first few times your shopping will take time but you will have fun to discover a new world in shopping and, believe me, it will pay back in taste alone.

One of my students, a prominent professor's wife, told me the following hint: With her left hand she touches the merchandise to be tested and in her right hand she holds the pendulum in a handmade, open mouthed, hangover satchel, so no one can see what she is doing.

I am enjoying the ingenuity of this lady and pass it on so that others may benefit from it.

Whenever you have a food allergy child or a member of your family is food allergic, the pendulum is more than handy!!

Often times one item by itself is good for a person but by combining several ingredients the delicate system of your beloved one cannot handle it and it becomes toxic to them. There is nothing wrong with the food by itself, it is the mixing of the different food vibrations that makes it difficult to digest for this particular person.

When your husband complains about an upset stomach, check what his stomach needs. In his left hand place your common household remedies like chamomile tea, peppermint tea, an antacid or vinegar water and watch the pendulum go. Give him what his vibration calls for and soon you have a happy and smiling husband again.

Check your clothes. Which dress is suited for today's task? Some fabrics affect your personal vibrations very much. Next time you go shopping, ask which fabric is good for my vibrations? Also ask, is it overpriced? Should I wait for a sale? You will have surprises all day long. There is never a dull moment in the universe.

Some of my students bring me contracts to be checked. They seem to have a fishy feeling about them.

When going over these contracts with the pendulum, ask:

"Which are the weak points in this contract?" The pendulum will stall over the parts to be redone. Sometimes it makes a negative motion altogether which means stay away from it all.

In business you can detect checks that are written under false pretense.

Go to your library and find the book which you should read at the present time by dangling the pendulum over the names of books.

When you go to a flower shop, pick the freshest flowers for your friends with the help of your pendulum.

Here is a good one and you should remember this. When you are injured in the wilderness, there is help within 300 feet circumference of the place where you are hurt. Employ your pendulum. Calm down and let God show you the way. There is a plant, a flower or a root to be placed on your injury. A pilot had heard my lectures on the pendulum. One evening he came into trouble. In a single engine plane he had an accident in icy conditions away from civilization. He calmed down and prayed. All at once he remembered the lecture and said "O.K., I will find help." In the snow he marked the directions north, south, east and west. Then he took his key as a pendulum and asked the Lord for help. Slowly, the pendulum showed northeast. He asked how many steps. It counted 165. The man dragged his injured feet the distance and found shelter from ice and snow in a cavern which was thickly covered with pine needles and dry leaves. He was recovered the next day without having received any frostbite or further injuries.

Always keep your questions simple. Ask for divine guidance. Then let go and let the great author of this world, the great mind, direct your words, your deeds and your steps and follow without questioning. You ask a question once. Be precise and to the point and that is enough.

Do not ask "Should I do this or that?"

"Should I write Mary or Ellen?"

"Should I drink this tea or that one?"

21

Also do not ask secrets of the universe. For example, in pregnancy do not ask "Will it be a boy?" "Will it be a girl?"

The pendulum is not a toy and not a means for predictions. It is an instrument for your survival. In this polluted world we have to have something to measure with. In the Bible it said measure "as in the days of old."

Every head of a household, man or woman, should be using this means of measurement to guide the family safely through the labyrinth of mistakes and dark forces.

In the hand of a religious, God trusting person the pendulum becomes a tool to speak to the Lord, to speak to the latent unseen powers in man which are of God.

You are a child of God.

You are a child of the universe.

The more you work with the pendulum, the keener your sixth sense will grow.

Everything of lasting value needs work. The musically gifted child has to practice and work to achieve his goal which is the complete control of an instrument in order to communicate with the divine for new harmonious creations or for perfect manifestations of harmony in sound.

You are reaching up now!!

"I will lift up mine eyes unto the hills, from whence cometh my help." Psalm 121:1

Workbook Pages

DOWSING EXERCISES

There are many methods of dowsing. Here are some dowsing exercises that illustrate some of these methods, as well as some questions that could be asked.

EXERCISE 1
(Yes / No Questions)

Get an organically grown fruit or vegetable as well as a conventionally grown fruit or vegetable and ask the following questions about each of them. Hold the fruit in your left hand (if you are right handed), or hold the fruit over your solar plexus (if you are left handed, thus leaving your left hand free to hold the pendulum.)

"Does this fruit have a toxin in it or on it?"

"Can this toxin be neutralized or removed?"

"If I soak the fruit in cider vinegar, will the toxin be removed?"

"If I set the fruit on a Soma Board for 10 minutes, will the toxin be neutralized?"

"If I eat this fruit, will the toxin harm my body?"

"Will this fruit taste good to me?"

"Is it safe for me to eat the fruit?"

(The answers to each of these questions should generate some other yes/no questions in your mind. Ask them.)

EXERCISE 2
(Measuring Energy Using a Fan Chart)

Use the fruits or vegetables from Exercise 1. Place each in turn in your left hand or hold at solar plexus as in Exercise 1. Hold the pendulum over the central point on the semicircular chart below and firmly make the following statement:

"Show me the energy of this fruit on a scale of 0 to 10 where 0 is the lowest and 10 is the highest energy."

You should find that the pendulum will slowly swing back and forth toward one of the numbers on the periphery of the semi-circle.

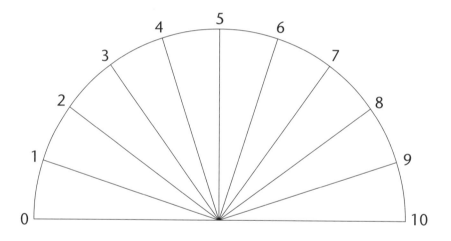

Exercise 2B: Try this exercise on your supplements. Besides asking if the supplements are beneficial to you (as in Exercise 1), ask to see the degree of benefit from 0 to 10.

Exercise 2C: Take a book you are reading and ask to be shown the level of Truth in it on a scale of 0 to 10. Also ask to see the overall Energy of the book on a scale of 0 to 10.

EXERCISE 3
(Permissions)

It is very important that we have permission at all levels before we dowse another person. For this exercise, write the names of four people on separate pieces of paper:

- Your name
- The name of a very close relative (Your mother, your husband, your child)
- The name of a politician who you don't know (Name of another country's leader)
- The name of a person who considers you as an enemy, or at least dislikes you.

Fold up each of the papers and place one at a time in the witness box found in the inside back cover of this book. As you hold the pendulum over the name and paper, ask the following questions:

"Am I capable of dowsing this person?"

"Do I have permission to dowse this person?"

"Is it to my highest good to dowse this person?"

You could be astonished by the answers. (If you get that you are not capable of dowsing for a person, you might want to consider a series of questions of why you are not capable. Too tired? Not enough experience? Too emotionally involved?)

THE 7 PHYSICAL CAUSES OF ILL HEALTH

1) Neglect

2) Trauma

3) Congestion

4) Toxins

5) Parasites

6) Infections

7) Miasma & Residues

Additional References

The 7 Spiritual Causes of Ill Health

26

EXERCISE 4
(Lists / 7 Physical & Spiritual Causes of Ill Health)

The next 11 pages consist of lists of potential health problems. Obtain two samples, one holding the vibration of yourself and another holding the vibration of a second person. You could use 'witnesses' such as saliva samples wrapped in plastic bags, hair samples, or pictures.

Use Exercise 3 to make certain that you have the necessary permissions and place the first sample in the witness box. Hold the pendulum over the sample as you point to each item on the list with your non-dominant hand. Firmly state the following:

"Show me a YES for the items on the lists that have priority health concern at this time for this person. Show me a NO for the items that are not of concern at this time for this person."

On the basis of each finding, navigate to subsequent lists for more details. If, for example, an item of priority concern is "Toxins," go to the "Toxin" list for specific chemical or metal toxicities.

Be sure to dowse the headings as well as the detail lines beneath the headings. For additional detailed lists as well as suggested remedies, use the lists in the book "Help One Another."

Cause #1 Neglect

Foods
    Food Combining
    Allergies or Food Sensitivities

Food Deficiencies
    Digestive Enzymes
    Amino Acids
    Cell Salts
    Minerals
    Vitamins
    Probiotics
    Other Food Deficiencies

Exercise
Fluorescent Lighting
Learning
Sleep
Water

Other Physical Neglect

Allergies and Food Sensitivities

Cheese	Perfume
Chocolate	Soy Products
Corn	Wheat
Eggs	Yeast Bread
Milk	Yogurt
MSG	Other
Orange	

Cause #2 Trauma

Accident

Blood Clots

Bones

Bruises

Clavicle

Difficult Birth

Displaced Organs

Operation

Radiation

Scar tissue

Shock

Short Circuit

Skin Trouble

Tailbone

Whiplash

Cause #3 Congestion

Adrenal Glands

Circulatory System

Blood

Brain

Bronchi

Colon

Gall Bladder

Kidneys

Liver

Lungs

Lymph

Magnetic Imbalance

Nerves

Pancreas

Pineal

Pituitary

Sinus

Spleen

Thyroid

Cause #4 Toxins

Chemical Poisons

Anthrax

Carbon Dioxide &
   Carbon Monoxide

Chem Trails

Dioxin

Food Additives

Food Irradiation

Formaldehyde

Nicotine

Nitrates & Nitrites

Pesticides

Pollution

Radiation

Stilbestrol

Mult. Chemicals

Metal Poisons

Aluminum

Arsenic

Asbestos

Cadmium

Copper

Gold

Graphites

Lead

Mercury

Nickel

Mult. Metals

Silver

Sulfur

Uranium

Cause #5 Parasites

1. Roundworms
Ancylostoma
Ascaris
Dog Heartworm
Hookworm
Pinworm
Strongyloides
Toxocara
Trichinosis
Vein Worm
Whipworm

2. Flatworms (Tapeworm Family)
Bladder Worm
Beef Tapeworm
Dog Tapeworm
Dwarf Tapeworm
Fish Tapeworm
Pork Tapeworm
Rat Tapeworm

3. Flatworms (Fluke Family)
Blood Flukes
Fish Flukes
Intestinal Flukes
Liver Flukes
Lung Flukes
Lymph Flukes
Pancreatic Flukes

4. Single Cell Parasites
Amoeba
Anaplasmosis
Cryptosporidium
Giardia
Leishmaniasis
Neospora
Protozoa
Sarcocystis
Spinal Fluid Parasites
Toxoplasmosis
Trichomonas

5. Spirochetes

Cause #6 Infections

1. Bacteria Infections
Diphtheria
Intestinal Bacteria
Staphylococcus
Strep

2. Fungus Infections
Cancer Fungus
Candida Fungus
Cryptomycosis
Maduromycosis

3. Virus Infections
Common Cold
Coxsackie Virus
Dog Virus
Epstein-Barr Virus
Hepatitis A
Hepatitis B

3. *Virus, cont.*
Hepatitis C
Herpes Virus
Influenza
Lenti Virus
Monomucleosis
Nerve Virus
Norwalk virus
Papilloma Virus
Retro-Virus
Simian 40 Virus
Sinus Infection
Spine 1 (8–100)
Spine 2 (82–00)
Spine 3 (88-88)
Spine 4 (88–100)

4. Viroid Infections

Cause #7 Miasma & Residues

1. Constrictors
Black Widow
Brown Spider
Crypto Fungus
Dog Bite
Insect Bite
Rattlesnake
Scorpion
Arscenic

2. Miasma
Congenital Defects
Cystic Fibrosis
Gonorrhea Virus
Malaria
Penicillin
Petrol Chemical
Radiation
Sickle Cell
Smallpox
Syphilis Spirochete
Tuberculosis Residue

3. Residues
Anthrax
Chickenpox
Diphtheria
Distemper
D.P.T.
Hepatitis B
Influenza
Measles
Mumps
Polio
Rabies
Rubella
Scarlet Fever
Smallpox
Tetanus
Whooping Cough
Yellow Fever

THE 7 SPIRITUAL CAUSES OF ILL HEALTH

1) Neglect

2) Trauma

3) Congestion

4) Karma

5) Entities & Dark Forces

6) Emotions

7) Law of the Universe

Emotions

Anger

Depression

Difficulty (Dealing With People)

Disappointment

Emotional Stability (Lack of)

Emotional Suffering (For Unknown Reason)

Fear

Hate

Interference (In Other People's Business)

Jealousy

Loss (Of a Loved One)

Mind Control

Suffering (From Financial Break)

35

Books by Hanna

"Wholistic health represents an attitude toward well being which recognizes that we are not just a collection of mechanical parts, but an integrated system which is physical, mental, social and spiritual."

Ageless Remedies from Mother's Kitchen

You will laugh and be amazed at all that you can do in your own pharmacy, the kitchen. These time tested treasures are in an easy to read, cross-referenced guide. (92 pages) ISBN: 1-883713-04-8

Allergy Baking Recipes

Easy and tasty recipes for cookies, cakes, muffins, pancakes, breads and pie crusts. Includes wheat free recipes, egg and milk free recipes (and combinations thereof) and egg and milk substitutes. (46 pages) ISBN: 1-883713-02-1

Alzheimer's Science and God

This little booklet provides a closer look by presenting Hanna's unique and religious perspectives. (15 pages) ISBN: 1-883713-10-2

Arteriosclerosis and Herbal Chelation

A booklet containing information on Arteriosclerosis causes and symptoms. (14 pages) ISBN: 1-883713-03-X

Cookbook for Electro-Chemical Energies

The opening of this book describes basic principles of healthy eating along with some fascinating facts you may not have heard before. The rest of this book is loaded with delicious, healthy recipes. A great value. (106 pages) ISBN: 1-883713-13-7

Free Your Body of Tumors and Cysts

Hanna brings together many natural techniques, including diet, herbs, vitamins, hands-on healing and more in a practical, understandable approach to growths and their relationships to parasites, cancer and leukemia. (77 pages) ISBN: 1-883713-18-8

God Helps Those Who Help Themselves

This work is a beautifully comprehensive description of the seven basic physical causes of disease. It is wholistic information as we need it now. A truly valuable volume. (196 pages) ISBN: 1-883713-11-0

Good Health Through Special Diets

This book shows detailed outlines of different diets for different needs. Dr. Reidlin, M.D. said, "The road to health goes through the kitchen not through the drug store," and that's what this book is all about. (90 pages) ISBN: 1-883713-14-5

Help One Another

It's the most complete compilation of Hanna's work to date; combining all the information from her 20 books with contributions from practitioners who worked closely with her. There are approximately 300 pages of Hanna's teachings on remedies, recipes, cleanses, foods, supplements and hands-on procedures. there is also an extensive index. A great resource! ISBN: 1-883713-19-6

How to Counteract Environmental Poisons

A wonderful collection of notes and information gleaned from many years of Hanna's teachings. This concise and valuable book discusses many toxic materials in our environment and shows you how to protect yourself from them. It also presents Hanna's insights on how to protect yourself, your family and your community from spiritual dangers. (53 pages) ISBN: 1-883713-15-3

Instant Herbal Locator

This is the herbal book for the do-it-yourself person. This book is an easy cross-referenced guide listing complaints and the herbs that do the job. Very helpful to have on hand. (109 pages) ISBN: 1-883713-16-1

Instant Vitamin-Mineral Locator

A handy, comprehensive guide to the nutritive values of vitamins and minerals. Used to determine bodily deficiencies of these essential elements and combinations thereof, and what to do about these deficiencies. According to your symptoms, locate your vitamin and mineral needs. A very helpful guide. (55 pages) ISBN: 1-883713-01-3

New Book on Healing

A useful reference book full of herbal, vitamin, food, homeopathic and massage suggestions for many common health difficulties. This book is up-to-date with Hanna's work on current health issues. (155 pages) ISBN: 1-883713-17-X

New Dimensions in Healing Yourself

The consummate collection of Hanna's teachings. An unequated volume that complements all of her other books as well as her years of teaching. (150 pages) ISBN: 1-883713-09-9

Old-Time Remedies for Modern Ailments

A collection of natural remedies from Eastern and Western cultures. There are more than 20 fast cleansing methods and many ways to rebuild your health. A health classic. (105 pages) ISBN: 1-883713-05-6

Parasites: The Enemy Within

A compilation of years of Hanna's studies with parasites. A rare treasure and one of the efforts to expose the truths that face us every day. (62 pages) ISBN: 1.883713-07-2

Spices to the Rescue

This is a great resource for how our culinary spices can enrich our health and offer first aid from our kitchen. Filled with insightful historical references. (64 pages) ISBN: 1-883713-12-9

Hanna's Books Published by Hay House

Healing with Herbs and Home Remedies A–Z

A compilation of *Ageless Remedies from Mother's Kitchen, Instant Herbal Locator, Instant Vitamin-Mineral Locator, New Book on Healing,* and *Spices to the Rescue.* (146 pages) ISBN 1-56170-795-3